OBSTACLE OVERCOMER

Motivate Yourself For A Victorious Life

ANJELA ANDERSON

authorHOUSE®

AuthorHouse™
1663 Liberty Drive
Bloomington, IN 47403
www.authorhouse.com
Phone: 1 (800) 839-8640

Published by AuthorHouse 05/17/2016

ISBN: 978-1-5246-0735-7 (sc)
ISBN: 978-1-5246-0734-0 (e)

Print information available on the last page.

This book is printed on acid-free paper.

CONTENTS

ENDORSEMENT

There is no doubt that God is using Anjela Anderson to help others in their journey of living a victorious life. In this book, *Obstacle Overcomer*, Anjela candidly shares her life story and testimony of being an overcomer despite many obstacles and challenges she faced in her life. This woman of God is a true testament of taking your trials and turning them into triumphs. This book will be a blessing to its readers, as it offers key tools that will help navigate you to a life of victory. I am confident that after you read each page, your faith will be renewed. Anjela Anderson has walked a journey of faith and she exemplifies it daily in her walk with Christ. I am confident that after you read this book, you too will be inspired to continue to walk by faith with a mindset of victory.

Bishop Paul S. Morton, Sr.
Founder, **Full Gospel Baptist Church Fellowship International**
Senior Pastor, **Changing A Generation Ministries, Atlanta, Georgia**
Overseer & Co-Pastor, **Greater St. Stephen Ministries, New Orleans, Louisiana**

INTRODUCTION

Dear Jamison,

As I sit here and begin to write my story, my life, and my testimony, I had you in mind. My first-born and eldest son, I write this book not just for others but to inform you that you have come from good, Godly ground. I want you to know that I am not only your mother, but your greatest supporter and biggest fan. My God-given role was not only to be a mother; God has saturated me on the inside to be different on the outside. In this autobiography, I want you to know who I am other than your mother—how I deeply feel and how I think, which is outside of the box and where I've been throughout my life. Also, how my life experiences have immensely affected me spiritually, mentally, and emotionally through my tests, trials, and triumphs.

You've enhanced my life and played a drastic role in who I am today. I have been molded and shaped by God but I have been positioned and set on the platform by you, my first-born (I will explain later in the chapters to come as you read). That Tuesday evening, January 20, 1987 at 7:02 PM, you graced my life, embraced my heart, and have forever inspired me to keep pushing, keep doing and keep moving in the direction I needed to go in. Your presence has always filled me intellectually. So I write this introduction to you in anticipation that you will digest who I truly am and where I'm going.

I heard you say not long ago that, "You are forever in debt for the hard work, dedication and structure I've provided for you in your life." Well, I'd like to say in closing that, it's been a complete and true honor to have experienced life you being my son."

Love,
Mom

"And he saith unto them, follow me and I will make you fishermen of men." - Matthew 4:19

INTRODUCTION II

Dear Quintin,

Before I gathered my writing tools today to write this letter to you, I began to think about you and what I was going to say. I thought about you this morning after I prayed and meditated. I want you to know how much I love you and desire the best for you. I want you to know how you've impacted my life in these last twenty-three years. As long as I have God in me, nothing will ever or could come against or destroy our journey, our test, and trials. Our journey has endured footprints of emotions and settled feelings throughout. In the process of writing this introduction, I felt your pain. All that you've gone through, endured, and the things that have been absent from your life, I feel. But, you are and forever will be more than a conqueror. I am your mother through Christ, your friend by the world, your motivator by what I speak to you, and I'm your confidant in spite of what people may say about you. I pray that you will receive this story, my life autobiography of how I have truly and finally found myself. Know that you have been a great part of that finding. I am not only your mother, but I am your friend too. I believe you will begin to see and know who I am as a person, and to you, as I speak through this book.

Son, I chose to give you life; in return, you have changed mine. For the better, I might add. I have also been through a tremendous amount of highs, like you, and have also had lows like you. Now, you will see and read in this autobiography of who I really am, why I still stand, why I'm existing, and why God has kept me through it all. Son, I ask that you open your eyes, clear your ears, sit back, indulge with meditation with the words you will read. It will explain why you, my second-born son, are here today. I thank God for you every day and the day you came into my life, Sunday, January, 10, 1993 at 4:54 AM. I love you wholeheartedly, Quintin.

Love,
Mom

"Yet, in all these things we are more than conquerors through him that loves us."
- Romans 8:37 (NKJV)

ACKNOWLEDGMENTS

I AM SO BLESSED AND GRATEFUL to so many awesome people that have steeped greatness and integrity into my life and to who have been so encouraging to me, which have inspired me to walk in my God-given destiny. Thank you to all that are responsible for developing me into the woman that I am today.

To my amazing parents: Mr. and Mrs. Donald and Mary Frances Wilson of Niles, MI, I could not have developed into the woman I am now without your guidance, corrections, teachings, sternness and most of all, your unconditional love. I am the result of your great parenting. Thank you for how and what you've instilled in me, my upbringing and the environment you kept me in made a difference. I will eternally honor you for your love, support, and blessings.

To my also-amazing parents: Mr. and Mrs. James and Shirley Anderson of Peoria, IL, your commitment to marriage and family is what I desire to follow. The example you continue to exemplify to so many others, gives me inspiration for years to come. I cannot tell you how blessed I feel for your acceptance, your unconditional love and your untiring support. I will forever be grateful for you.

Thank you to my two sons: Jamison L. Ware and Quintin J. Pegross, I could not have written this book without you two. You have taught me uncounted lessons and I am so blessed how you both have graced my life. The motherhood platform I hold today is only because of you. I could not imagine life without sons such as you. It has been an honor to be your mother. I am thankful to my family for your prayers as I touch the lives of God's people.

To my two sisters: Patricia McDonald, of Indianapolis, Indiana and Carol Carter, of St. Paul, Minnesota, Thank you for the way you've embraced me over the recent years, encouraged me in the word of God, and been examples of great leadership, being the leading ladies that you are and how you have shown me what a Godly woman should look like and be.

GRATITUDE OF THANKS

Overseer Gregory James, Life Church International Center, Tallahassee, Florida

Mother Marjorie Simon, Changing A Generation FGBC, Atlanta, Georgia

Sis. Jannalyn Davis, Executive Assistant to Bishop Paul Morton, Changing A Generation FGBC, Atlanta, Georgia

Changing A Generation FGBC

Changed Women at CAG

Jamison L. Ware

Quintin J. Pegross

Ms. Brittany Tilford

My grandchildren, Ta'lon Ware and Milan Ware

SPECIAL THANK YOU

Bishop Paul S. Morton, Sr. and Dr. Debra B. Morton

I would like to express my sincere and heartfelt gratitude of an extraordinary thank you to my amazing pastor and co-pastor, my Spiritual Leaders, Bishop Morton and Pastor D. God has truly set you apart for greater! The work that God has done and is doing through you is absolutely astonishing. You have poured so much into my life in ways I could never imagined—with your ministry, your leadership, and for the Kingdom. I've learned so much from your teachings, your God-given instructions and your integrity. You have blessed me immensely. My household is better because of the dominion series you have taught being under your leadership. You demonstrate and teach so profoundly with the Spirit of Excellence and with the humility you behold, I am forever inspired. Again, thank you Bishop Morton and Pastor D, for showing God's people how to be Kingdom Representatives! I Love You Always!

Anjela Anderson, HTA

PREFACE

As I introduce to some and present to others, I, Anjela greet you in Divine Love. I do not take it lightly the fact that I have captured your attention to this book. I will not take your time for granted; what I will do is bless you and lead you down the right path to conquer your inabilities to become a winner. In the midst of doing so, you will regain your confidence and be enlightened in a peaceable and spirit-filled way. My story, my life, and this book are called to be an inspirational journey.

In this autobiography, I pray you will receive the knowledge and integrity to enhance of knowing who you are and whose you are. You the reader, the woman who has fallen victim to others, not knowing who, she really is. The woman who has been a caretaker to others but not cared for herself, who has not felt accepted by her family, peers, or society. To the one who has nurtured life but not the life of her own person. The woman who feels that she has never fit in with anything but has always believed in everything. I pledge to inspire you, to motivate you, and believe that you will begin to take, be and stay in control of your life.

I have stories to inspire you. So no matter what you may endure in life, the obstacles you've had to overcome, mountains you've had to climb, valleys you've had to jump over, you'll be just fine and will remain sane. If you don't see the light right now, know that *there is* a light at the end of the tunnel. It's there and shining bright, waiting for you!

In the end, stay encouraged, know who you represent—God—and always believe. Believing is receiving.

FOREWORD

I feel honored, privileged and most of all blessed to be connected to, a part of, and writing for my sister, Anjela D. Anderson's, book. First and foremost, Anjela is a God-fearing woman who loves the Lord. Anjela's natural and spiritual beauty shines from the inside out. Furthermore, Anjela's voice, charismatic style, and caring and humble spirit are gifts from God. Generally, sisters are each other's best friend while growing up, but Anjela and I didn't meet each other until twelve years ago.

However, it seems as I've known her all my life. I learned from our relationship in a short time that it's not the quantity of time that you've known a person, but the quality of your relationship which makes it genuine. God meditated our relationship and we have been close ever since we met at my 50th birthday celebration. You may not remember what a person says or does, but you will remember how a person makes you feel. Anjela made me feel very special to attend my birthday celebration in the cold weather of Minnesota during the month of January and she will make you feel special as well in her own way.

Anjela's testimony of her life will make you reflect on yourself or someone you know but most of all inspire you through her journey of life. The cliché "everything that glitters isn't gold" can be identified in this book about her life. She has faced some very challenging and hurtful things from the people closest to her. Anjela has raised two African-American sons predominantly by herself with the guidance of God. Anjela is hard-working and pursues the best in what and who she engages her time with. Anjela's experience as a daughter, sister, mother, aunt and friend shared in this book may help someone to see they can make it too. Anjela is beautiful, strong, dedicated and an intelligent woman of God who has survived tough times, but she has endured it all by God's grace and mercy.

I challenge you to enjoy this book with laughter, tears, an open heart, and open mind. Everything happens in God's time, in his way and for his purpose. Therefore, if you are reading this book it's not by coincidence or accident but because of God's plan. "For I know the plans I have for you, declares the Lord, plans to prosper you and not harm you, plans to give you hope and a future" (Jeremiah 29:11) I give God the praise and the glory for his gift he has given his child and my sister, Anjela D. Anderson.

With Much Love,

Carol Anderson Carter

ABOUT THE AUTHOR

Anjela was born Angela Denise Boykin on November 16, 1966 in Peoria, Illinois to Henry Alfred and Mary Frances Boykin. Anjela graduated from high school in June of 1985 in South Bend, Indiana. On September 6, 1988 she relocated to Tacoma, Washington with her twenty-one-month-old and gifted son, Jamison. She remained a single parent, worked in a variety of medical facilities, hospitals and nursing homes to make ends meet for herself and her son. She went onto college and studied at Tacoma Community College to go into the nursing and medical fields which were her first loves. Anjela gave birth to another son, Quintin, in 1993, whom she adores. Although she desires to marry one day, she is currently a single and focused woman.

It was relocating to Tacoma, Washington as a single parent and woman living thousands of miles away from her immediate family that boosted her stature of maturity. She also gives tribute to her beloved and late sister, Belinda Jean Mikell, for presenting her the opportunity and benefaction to relocate to another part of the country to explore her potential. She now recognizes that was her ticket to success that gave her and her sons a grounded foundation and greater influenced life. She later moved to Indianapolis, Indiana and to the Washington, DC area where she accepted work assignments and continued to work in the medical field.

In May of 2008, after years of unhappiness, struggles, hardships, and disappointments, she packed up her vehicle with only her clothes, personal items, and a few thousand dollars and moved to Atlanta, Georgia where she currently resides. Anjela resides in Northwest Atlanta where she is now enjoying life with her two beautiful grandchildren and living comfortably in a quiet retirement community and credits God for supplying her every need.

OVERCOMER'S PRAYER

Dear Heavenly Father, I come before you on today thanking you for your grace and mercy and everlasting kindness. I ask that you take me to a place as I indulge into this inspirational journal. Take me to the place where I need to be to overcome every obstacle in my life. Take me to where I'm no longer looking at the mountains I face, but to where I can look down over them. Renew my mind, clear my heavy heart, humble myself and open my ears to hear what thus says the Lord. I pray I will receive your counsel and your eternal wisdom through your son, Jesus Christ, through Obstacle Overcomer.

In Jesus Name,
Amen

Chapter One

THE BEGINNING

JOHN 10:27

In the beginning, there was a little brown-skinned girl; her name was Angie. It all began on one Sunday afternoon in 1974, when Angie was eight years old. This little girl always had two little ponytails on each side of her head, because the pink foam rollers with the pink hard plastic snaps never fully curled her hair. This caused her bangs to always be half curled in the front of her forehead. The back of her head was flat and matted down because she didn't have enough hair to fit in rubber bands to put in a ponytail. She wore laced white dress socks, which folded down neatly around her little ankles with her black patent leather shining shoes with a big gold buckle in the middle. She had on her navy blue striped dress with a white ruffled blouse tucked inside. She was a cute little girl, or so she thought. After getting out of church that day, she and her siblings got into the car parked on the side of the curb. She recalls being the last one to get into the car on the passenger side as her mother stood outside, talking to one of the church members as she configured a way for all her children to fit into the car.

Angie resented being the last one to get in the car, being that she was next to the youngest out of ten brothers and sisters. Before she could get in the car, she heard a voice, but it wasn't a human's voice. It was an internal, yet she felt it coming from another place. It was soft and it purified her mind like no other voice she had ever heard from a human. It was God's voice. Her inner spirit was calm, something that she had never felt before. This voice was so surreal, dreamlike, and unearthly. It was as if she was in a dream standing right there on the street curb. As her Mother, Frances was standing by the car it was then that Angie said to her, "I just had a conversation with God" and that "God just spoke to me." She remembers him saying, "I love you and you're going to be different and I'm wrapping my arms around you." Her mother did acknowledge the fact that the Lord had just visited her little girl. After her encounter with God for the first time, she doesn't remember communicating with God or being in contact with him anymore until she was 13 years of age.

In between those years, my family moved to two different cities. I was in ballet and gymnastics. I remember in my early teenage years when I started going to church on a regular basis. Although I didn't like to sing, I sung in the choir. My mother made me sing in the choir and made me go to church. Clearly, I didn't have a choice in the matter, but I thank God for it being so and an open discussion now. After attending church regularly, I didn't mind going because it felt good when I was there but after church was over and being back at home, I felt unattached from God and somewhat unloved by my family.

Chapter Two

MY LIFE

LUKE 6:28 KJV

I grew up in a big family of eleven children. I was the ninth child to be born, and the youngest of my mother's six daughters. As I waited for an answer of who my natural father was, I never received it at the time of growing up. Sometimes in life, your answer may not come when you want it to come or think when it should come. But in May 2004, it all came to an end. The end of always wondering where I came from. If you keep focus, keep moving forward and fasting in prayer, your breakthrough shall come. It may not come in the way we planned, but God will format it in the way He will have it to be. I always knew there was something different with my being. Not in a bad way, but just different. Not only was I treated differently but I looked different too. My hair was not long like the rest of my sisters. My skin tone complexion was more of a bronze color. I had a well-toned body, even as a little girl, with big legs and shapely muscle calves, unlike my sisters. My breasts were very large at an early age and were bigger than the average teenager. I didn't understand why and how the youngest daughter, such a young girl, could have the biggest of everything. It definitely made me feel awkward.

One Saturday morning, I was ironing my clothes for school on Monday. Back then, I always got my clothes ready on the weekend and prepared them for the upcoming school week. Other siblings were around doing what we normally did on Saturdays, watched TV, played in the living room or just sat around and listened to grown folks' conversation. For some reason, I must have made a family member mad about something, because out the blue she started asking me if I was having sex. Yes, having sex! More or less, she was accusing me of having sexual relations.

I could not configure why she asked me this because I don't remember giving her any reason or any evidence to assume this. I began telling her that I was not having sex. At that time I *was* attracted to boys, but I was a cheerleader too and cheerleading was my main focus. I was not going to let anything come between that. I asked her several times to please stop accusing me and to move away from me. She kept at the accusations and started telling me that she would whip my butt and saying things like, "You know that a boy's penis doesn't have to go all the way in and all it has to do is just be at the tip of the vagina" that I can get pregnant that way too.

I looked at her in a way that said, *can you please move so I can finish ironing my clothes?* During that time, I truly did not know why she was so hard on me, and wanting to know if I was sexually active. My mother never accused me of having sex, so I often wondered why she did. So, by the third round of her accusations, I promised her and began screaming at her that if she didn't stop accusing me and get away from me, that I would throw the hot iron I had in my hand at her, just so she would stop nagging me about having sex.

As I grew up and got older, she was the main one who always mistreated me. As an adult, every time I would come around or walk into a conversation she was in, she would cut her conversation short, or move away from me to the other side of the room as if I was contaminated, or as if she didn't want me to touch her. I didn't know why she acted like that then, but I do now. I truly believe she saw something different in me; I believe she sensed the oil, the anointing of God on my life.

As I grew into adulthood, she repeatedly displayed her indignity toward me and it also spilled over onto my oldest son and my grandson. She treats my oldest son and I differently to this day. As I write this book, she only communicates with my youngest son. To my knowledge, she only communicates with him because my youngest son and I were at odds with each other at one time. My analogy to this is: the enemy is always going to side with, relate to, and correlate with the spirit, that the stronghold has gone against, God's spirit. Spirits identify with one another and gravitate towards one another of the same spirit. On the other hand, my oldest son has always had his mother's back. He's the one that has always respected me to the utmost, never a foul word has come from him toward me. He has always treated me with loving kindness, dignity and with honor. So, just like grease and water can't stick together, neither can evil and good. Therefore, She doesn't acknowledge my grandchildren being that they're a part of me. Sadly, I still do not have a relationship with this family member today. After several attempts, I have tried to reach out to her and have ask for forgiveness although I don't know what I was asking forgiveness for, she refuses to this day. She will not communicate with me or even let me know as to why she refuses to talk to me. One day God said to me, "Anjela, you have done your part, now let me do my part." I get so excited when God says He's going to do His part. But one thing I do know is that, it is not she herself, but it's the spirit she allows to live within her.

"For the flesh desires what is contrary to the Spirit, and the Spirit what is contrary to the flesh. They are in conflict with each other, so that you are not to do what you want." (Galatians 5:17) "For I know good itself does not dwell in me, that is, in my sinful nature. For I have the desire to do what is good, but I cannot carry it out." (Roman 7:18 NIV)

Because the true living God and the Holy Spirit will not allow a person to be and act as such with un-forgiveness or evil, or go without forgiving one another. In Psalm 5:4 NASB it states: "For you are not a God who takes pleasure in wickedness; No evil dwells with you." We all know that God is Love and He is a forgiving God, right? Yes He is. So, as much as it may hurt, I must continue to pray for her. That someday, God will resurrect her heart and deliverance will take place and saturate her spirit, that is my prayer. I love her dearly and have washed the past away into the Sea of Forgetfulness. I have moved forward and moved on. But now as I look back over my life, I understand why I was mistreated.

I share this story because it's this type of treatment that can affect someone, as it has affected me to a certain point. Although it did affect me, it didn't control me nor did it make me who I am today. But she always made me feel that I didn't belong in my family and disconnected from my other siblings, all because of her actions. I carried this unsettling feeling with me for many years. But one day I decided to make a change for the better. One day God handed me a petition. He said, Anjela, there is nothing wrong with you and "You are fearfully and wonderfully made: marvelous are thy works; and your soul knoweth right well." (Psalm 139: 14)

After that encounter, I made sure that I was not going to allow myself to suffer and trap myself in bondage from one person's downfalls. I could have fallen in the devil's camp, but I refused to and you can to. The camp of depression, insecurities, and not knowing who I was, but in God! This is why it is so imperative to show genuine love, be fair to one another, judge not your neighbor and be kind to one another—because it's situations like these that can tear families and relationships apart. Then we wonder why women today are at each other's temples. It's because when our older generation of women do not demonstrate and show the younger women, our female family members, and loved ones, women that are coming up behind them today in which they should be looking up to them, in admiration, being positive role models and powerful women in the Lord. The scripture says, "Likewise, teach the older women to be reverent in the way they live, not to be slanders or addicted to much wine, but to teach what is good. Then they can urge the younger women to love their husbands and children." (Titus 2:3,4 NIV)

IN WHICH I CAME?

In May 2004, it all came to an end—the end of wondering whence I came. I was living in the Midwest; I drove 210 miles to meet my biological Dad, for the very first time! My late Uncle, who was the brother of my believed-to-be-Dad whom I though was my biological father until the age of sixteen. My uncle assisted and helped me set up the meeting arrangement with my biological Dad who had agreed to meet me. I know and truly believe that God was in the midst of this reunion and allowed us to come together. Everything was ready to be put on the table. So I packed up my two sons; my brother and his wife, and my sister and her husband traveled with me for moral support. We all followed each other in three cars. Once I entered into the city, my heart began to pump harder and beat much faster. I knew I was getting ready to meet the missing link to my life. I was finally ready to see and meet my biological dad, the man I had heard so much about. The man that I heard was a great provider, along with his great looks.

My Uncle and I rode around the city in his car looking for my dad. We went through a couple of alleys that he was known to hang out in with his buddies. They were there, but my dad wasn't. So about thirty minutes had passed of searching for him but we couldn't find him. Yes, of course, doubt started to set in. I began to think that he had changed his mind about meeting me and didn't want to go forth with the meeting. After looking for my dad for about an hour my Uncle and I decided to go back to his house because I didn't want to be looking for a man who knew this was the day he was supposed to meet his daughter, with knowing that we were supposed to meet. We pulled up to my Uncle's house and there was my dad's car in my uncle's driveway!

I got out the car and walked around the house into the backyard and he was sitting at the table. Wow! He looked at me, I looked at him and it was magical! We hugged, talked, and laughed down to memory lane. Throughout the fellowship and gathering that day, I often captured him staring at me several times and he caught me staring at him. I believe we both were truly relieved that this had finally happen and it was over too. That we finally met after thirty-seven years! We began to talk and reminisce about our life in the past. He told me about his mother passing away shortly ago, his other children, my siblings which he had three other daughters and one son. My dad and I look exactly alike. I will admit I stared him down because our smile, our teeth, lips, hands, fingers, our demeanor and even our body language were exactly alike. I was definitely his twin and he was most certainly my twin!

I know I am blessed because stories like these rarely happen and not very often. In 2016, I am now proudly an Anderson! It had to be the power of God that touched my Anderson Family. It all began with my sister from my Dad's side who has reached out to me like you wouldn't believe. We have grown very close since reuniting with my dad. My second Mother, my dad's beautiful wife, has just been amazing and unbelievable. I've truly tried to side with her and put myself in her shoes, but I simply cannot fit into them. How she did it, how she have accepted me, embraced me and acknowledges me as her daughter, with no questions asked. I've carefully watch her and she doesn't refer to me as her "stepdaughter;" she introduces me as her "daughter." What a wonderful feeling and a wonderful woman of God she is. I'm assuming she never knew anything about me until 2004 after being married to my dad since 1968. She lived her life; her family had been established, she raised her children, almost to retirement, she had grandchildren, she had a life of her own. Then, her life was interrupted by me.

It had to be the power of God and the blood of Jesus that touched her heart, mind, and soul for embracing me and welcoming me into her life, her home, and her family. And with that I will be forever grateful, love and respect her to the utmost and hold her name up to the Lord. If it was not for the Lord, and secondly, my Anderson Family where would I be? God and the Anderson's helped me and held me up through the roughest times in my life. God is a Keeper and my Fortress. The Anderson's have been my keepsake. Why? Because family shows it. That's what The Anderson's have been for me.

In January 2011, I flew to St. Paul, Minnesota to meet my new sister. After meeting her, things took off like a speeding bullet. Our relationship flourished and sprouted out like a flower. She is my prayer partner today. She encourages me in my daily walk with the Lord and in my dark days too. My relationships with all of my Anderson siblings have grown beautifully; it has been a beautiful breakthrough. Sadly, I don't have a genuine brotherly and sisterly relationship with some of the siblings I grew up. It remains unsettled, but through the grace of God, this too shall pass.

> "I will prepare a table before you in the presence of your enemies and anoint your head with oil, let your cup overflow and run over" (Psalm 23:5)

~ What God is saying in *Psalm 23:5* is he will allow your enemies and foes to look at you in a straight line and see how you're being lifted up by Him from afar, where they are, to see you, and how God has enlarged your territory and moved you into greater.

> "I will make your enemies your footstools." (Luke 20:43)

~ What God is saying in *Luke 20:43* is he will make your enemies witnesses to where you are going. For all they have put you through, how they have set back and watched you as the devil tried to make you stumble. He will allow all of them, every last one of them, including the devil, to behave a certain way, just to get you in a divine place, your place of destiny.

WORDS OF ENCOURAGEMENT

I used to wonder why people, especially women would stare at me, not include me in certain things, their conversations, activities, I would never get invitations to their social gatherings. Well, God's revelation came to me all at once in December 2013. It wasn't me per say, but it was the God in me. It was God's anointing on my life, it was evident. It was his anointing that shined on me and through me. They could clearly see something different in me, God's Glory. God said in His word that we are a peculiar people, we are *supposed* to be different and we are *not* to fit in and in certain partakings. God will surely raise you up and put you on display. He'll let you stand out. He'll let His light shine through you, for His purpose and His purpose only. He will even make you look different, appear different, carry yourself different, be perceived differently and ultimately be different in every way altogether.

At one previous employer, I would get stares and snares from my co-workers every day. I knew that I carried myself professionally and respectfully, I spoke well and was spoken well of. My patients would tell me from time to time that I had great mannerisms unlike some of my co-workers they had encountered. But little did my sweet patients and haters know that this didn't all come on just yesterday or came at me instantly. As a child of God, you will indeed experience mistreatment. It may be at the workplace, in your family, in the church and in society's world. Jesus was persecuted and you will be too. But continue to walk in your destiny. Remember, we are a peculiar people and expect to be treated and looked at different. It's okay, because we are *not* supposed to look like the world anyway; we are even supposed to *look* different. There's a certain glow that others won't have. People should look at you and notice that there is something is different about you. There's a special anointing and glow that should be on your life and your lips. "We are in the world but not of the world" (John 17:16) Remember, you cannot effect change where you blend in. You're going to face some challenges and some persecutions. Remember, God's light has shined on you now and you no longer belong to the world. You belong to your Father now. You will face being treated different than your co-workers.

Here's a true story that I endured one time at the workplace. I was having lunch one day in the break room. This co-worker of mine had to sit next to me because all of the other chairs were occupied. But it was quite obvious that she didn't want to eat next to me. She moved all of her belongings on the table that were near my belongings. She made sure that she removed her silverware, her food, was far away from my food, her drink, her lunch bag and she even went as far as scooting her chair over away from me although she still sat next to me. She didn't want absolutely anything on the table of hers touching mine that belonged to me. This woman did not want to sit next to me for the life of her! Can you imagine all this just because you want to eat your lunch? Yes, this actually happened to me! But if she really knew what was for her good, she'd allow everything of hers to touch everything of mine! Bless them O Lord. Jesus said, "Father forgive them, for they do not know what they are doing, and they divided up his clothes by casting lots" (Luke 23:34) So not only did God set me apart from the world but he also set me apart from the women I worked with because of their actions and the differences they displayed toward me. It was really bad, just awful. I was very hurt when they would show this type of behavior toward me. But these are the persecutions you endure when you turn your life over to the Lord.

I was so set apart that even when I walked up to them while they were in a group talking. As soon as I would present myself in their presence, the talking amongst them would cease and they'd scatter amongst themselves and individually went about their work day. They simply didn't want me around; they surely and clearly let me know. Whenever this would happen, I would reflect on these Scriptures:

> "Now the Lord is the Spirit: and where the Spirit of the Lord is, there *is* liberty" (2 Cor 3:17 KJV)

> "When God arise, let his enemies be scattered; let him that also that hate him flee before him" (Psalm 68:1 KJV).

The Lord will allow His Spirit to rise up and show up on the scene anywhere and anytime because He *is* everywhere. The reason why she didn't want me touching her things and they didn't want me around is because when the anointing is on your life and you are in the midst of confusion, cliques, backbiting, jealousy, envy and unclean spirits, it breaks and destroys yokes (Isaiah 10:27 KJV) And when the power of God is present, things must change. So, all who are tested and treated as such, be encouraged!

When you study, eat and drink the Word of God daily and allow your flesh to die daily He keeps you even you don't want to be kept. So be sure to keep God's Commandments hidden in your heart and always keep a sacrificial offering unto God. If not, our sinful man will have the tendency and surely rise up to try and satisfy what our flesh desires rather than what God desires for us. So we must keep our flesh under subjection to Christ and the written law of His word. People fail to realize that church folks are human too. We are always in transformation like everyone else. We're people first, then we are Christians. Remember we are all born again, sinners saved by grace. Meaning we were all born into a sinful world, have done sinful things, sinful activities. No one, including me, is exempt from this status. So sin has lived in us longer than are renewed bodies. This is why it's so important to submit our bodies as a living sacrifice, holy and acceptable unto Christ Jesus.

Don't let me fool you now, please know that I was a work in progress. It took time for me, for God to transform my life, my ways, my heart, me as a person and as a woman. So, please don't get it twisted because I was not always the woman you see now. Women seem to always judge other women by the way they look, and never try to understand truly where she came. What she had to go through, the path that she had to walk, the steps she had to climb, the hurdles she had to jump through, the stumbles, the falls and the road she had to go down. The trials she had to endure, the fires she had to face. So until you're ready and willing to face the fire and literally go through everything and more than the one that you're judging or looking at in a dismantled way, don't judge. Because you don't know what she had to go through to get where she is now. Life is real and it's not going to stop for you or me.

It is God who chooses certain people to face certain situations so they can tell of His goodness; I know he chose me. So when people such as; family members, people you thought were your friends, so-called friends ("frenemies") and your enemies stop socializing, speaking and talking to you – count it all joy. You may not know why or fully understand what is going on during the time of the separation or the gap of communication as to why their doing the things they're doing but I'm here to tell you, it's going to be all for your good. God will put you in the midst of your enemies, the ones who have hate towards you and people that don't have your best interest at heart. He does this so that He can put you on His platform. And once you're on God's platform, no one can knock you off.

So after you endure all the abuse from people, God says, that's enough. Now it's time for Him to put you up on the mantle, His display, in His realm and bring you out of your storm, your heartache and pain. You're going to look better than you did before, you're going to look extraordinaire. So I don't care what it seems like, looks like, or what it feels like, just stand. It is working together for your good. You may feel at times you've been knocked down, stepped on, rolled up and twisted up but when God gets through with you and brings you out, the world will surely know it.

Chapter Three

THE EMBRACEMENT

ROMANS 10:10

There have been numerous times in my life where I didn't know where to go, to whom or where to turn, to but I soon found out. I had to turn to God, no question about that. If you dwell in your affliction long enough, God will surely bring you out of it and bring it to past. He will bring you out of any situation that you find yourself in. It may not be when you want or think you should be brought out but I assure you it will be in God's perfect timing. Sometimes, God will leave you in that thing, that situation, as long as he needs to in order to transform, cleanse and mold you. Believe me, when he transforms you and when the transforming is over, you'll know it and so will others.

God is not about lack or slack, so when He gets ready to put you on His showcase to show His people what you've had to endure, he will bring you out shining as white as snow. He will make it as if you haven't gone through anything. People will not recognize who you are through your testimony of telling them what you went through or the trials you had to endure. They'll look at you in disbelief or as if it's unbelievable. See that's the kind of God we serve. God is bigger than our little problems. We think our problems are big, but they're really small to God. There's no problem, situation or circumstance that we have in our lives that God cannot handle. THERE IS NOTHING TOO HARD FOR GOD. GOD CAN DO ANYTHING!

Speaking of God can do anything, my Anderson family has been one of the best things that has happened to me in my life. They have helped me through some tough times. I say this because after the passing of my mother in 2008 and my sister in 2009, my family and siblings that I grew up with definitely grew apart. Understandably so; I'm sure we were all hurt, in pain, and grieving too. This was a traumatic time in all of our lives but we should have come together as a family even more. Honestly, I don't know what drew us apart the way it did. After having your mother and sister pass away so close together is tough alone in itself to deal with. But God is a Sustainer, He's a Keeper, and a Comforter. I believe we tried to handle it in our way or the best way we could.

I say that God can do anything because my Anderson family continually "embraced" me during this time. I didn't understand how they could be there for me the way that they were without knowing me very well. But God! They called, checked up on me, texted me, encouraged me and prayed with me when they didn't have to, but I know it was that God touched their hearts. Sadly, the mistreatment started again in 2011 with the same family member I spoke about in chapter two, but it was all for my good. I know the mistreatment was the result of me having a different father. I often heard from some of my older siblings throughout my life that the last name I carried was not of the man believed to be my father. I was told I was conceived through infidelity. Even if I was, so what? I was here now and I was not going anywhere, I was here to stay. At this point I still do not have a full understanding of why I'm still being mistreated by this same family member? But what the devil meant for evil, God turned it around for my good. I would not be here if God didn't allow it. There was and is a purpose for me and for my life because I'm here. If you are here on earth and breathing, there's a reason for your life. Whether it was by natural birth, cesarean section, or however you got here, you are meant to be here! Never think that your mistakes, your shortcomings or your reason being here on earth is a void. There's a reason for every living creature, we just have to reach deep down inside and search for it, and pull it out.

As God began to move in my life, using me for His glory and elevating me to other levels in Him, I also began to acquire haters. God began to do a work in me, and they surely witnessed it. You must be aware that people will not always be happy for you. Get over it, they're not going to be excited for you like you think they should or want them to be.

Unfortunately, you cannot share your blessings with everyone. You have to be strategic with who you share your God-given talents with. There are under-handed people, haters, and evildoers that do not and will not have your best interest at heart. They'll never be sincere for your happiness. Jealousy, envy, and strife will begin to set in from the people closest to you. So, please don't expect everyone to rejoice with you in a triumph. But when you rejoice in others and their blessings, you are opening doors for yourself for God to bless you. It is then when your blessings will be released in your life. It has worked for me and I know it will work for you. I try at every opportunity when someone is being blessed, has a blessing to share with me or is in a joyous state in their life to be genuinely happy and have sincere happiness toward them. Just by me rejoicing in someone else's blessings, God will indeed bless me and enlarge my territory.

That is for sure one way to block your blessing, God's blessings. His blessings are different than an approval from man. However, promotions come from God, not man. God's promotions last a lifetime; a handout from man is temporary and may not last until the next day, let alone the next hour. God's blessings, miracles, and promotions always outlast anything else and will never be taken back.

Chapter Four

THE STEPS TO SUCCESS

PHILIPPIANS 4:13 NIV

Success can and may come in different ways, shapes and forms. It is described as a person or thing that achieves, desires, aims, or attains prosperity. Your success is directly connected to what you have in your hands. What happens in your hands may not happen in someone else's hands. For example, if a bank or financial institution turns you down or rejects you for that loan you have asked God for. Just use these words, "Well I'm going to another bank and God said 'He shall supply all of my needs according to his riches in glory by Christ Jesus' (Philippians 4:19 KJV) So, what the natural can't and won't do for you, the supernatural power of God can.

God's word, God's way, and *your* faith will do it for you. When the financial institutions offer you the very best deal, that tips the scale that they have that's because God was strategically involved in the process. When you trust God you will elect Him to move on your behalf, but you have to trust Him with all your heart. God will always be ready to move on your behalf and perfect that which concerns me; Your mercy, O Lord, *endures* forever; Do not forsake the works of your hand (Psalm 138:8) But only when you place your trust totally in Him.

Sometimes God may not allow it to work out as you would desire because He sees behind the scenes; He sees what we cannot see. God is all knowing and He knows what's for our good, as for us on the other hand, we only see the present. God knows all, is all and sees our future. He knows the end from the beginning, the beginning from the end, so be patient; He has something much greater in stored for you which is on the other side of the table. Put it in God's hand

and release it from yours. When you do that, it'll be a guaranteed assurance that greater is waiting.

THINKING POINTS - IT DEPENDS ON WHOSE HAND IT'S IN

My Hands: Not Enough.
God's Hands: More Than Enough.

TRUE SUCCESS PRODUCES ENEMIES:

People are not going to like you. Get over it. They will try to find out where you're going, and beat you there, what you have and how much but not have a heart for you. They are waiting to see you fall, because they have; and they're waiting for you to get there. You're going to have some haters, jealous folks and people that want to see you lose it all. People will pretend to like and support you. You'll see it because they'll get silent towards you and stop speaking and talking to you.

But if they do talk to you, it will small talk. Why will it be small talk? Because their spirit and heart are not agreeing where God is taking you and they see how God is blessing and elevating you. You will know exactly who they are because God will confirm it. You're going to face some isolation. You're going to feel alone and be alone too, but being alone is good for you because it's all in God's plan. Not only will isolation be good for you, but it's going to mold you and humble you for your next assignment. So get ready, it's coming! When you begin to go higher in your calling your enemies will not be able to handle your success. The devil will surely invite you into his recess. Be careful who you accept invitations from, who you surround yourself with and who you keep in your company. The gossip, the lies and the hate will begin. But you've got to keep pressing on until the end. Again, when you reach new levels in Christ, and during the elevation. That is not the time to receive praise and thanks from people but that will be the time to be in prayer and ask to be prayed for. That will be the toughest time because the devil will be out to attack you any way he can, especially through the people you thought were your friends. The bigger you prevail in God, the bigger the demons will be.

THE FOUR STEPS TO SUCCESS:

1) HAVE A HIGH AGENDA
2) **YOUR FAITH** (You must believe in God)
3) GREAT ENERGY
4) PERSEVERANCE: GOD IS THE MASTER OF MULTIPLICATION

A HIGH AGENDA: Keep your standards high. If a subject or plan is at the top of someone's agenda, it is the most important thing they want to discuss. Discuss your success with successful people.

FAITH: Faith is defined as belief with strong conviction; firm belief in something for which there may be no tangible proof; complete trust, confidence, reliance or devotion. Faith is the opposite of doubt.

ENERGY: Is the ability to do work, or the ability to move or elicit change in matter. In effect, the amount of energy something has refers to its capacity to cause things to happen.

PERSEVERANCE: Steadfastness in doing something despite difficulty or delay in achieving success.

Synonyms: persistence, tenacity, determination, staying power.

FAITH FACTS: "You must have FAITH." – Hebrews 11:1 KJV "Now faith is the substance of things hoped for, the evidence of things not seen."

The word "substance" translated in Greek means "a placing or setting under a substructure or foundation." This word appears elsewhere in the New Testament as "Confident" or "Confidence" (2 Corinthians 9:4 and Hebrews 3:14 KJV) The word "evidence" comes from the Greek term "elegchos" which means: a proof or that by which a thing is proved or tested; conviction.

FAITH (N): Complete trust or confidence in someone or something.

Synonyms – Trust, belief, confidence, conviction, optimism (hopefulness), hope

A Strong belief in God or in the doctrines of a religion, based on spiritual apprehension rather than proof.

(Faith Synonyms (In relation to) – Religion, church, denomination, religious) persuasion, (religious) belief, ideology, creed, teaching, doctrine.

The context in question deals with the existence of the universe. For Hebrews 11:3 says, "Through faith we understand that the worlds were framed by the word of God, so that the things which are seen were not made of things which do appear." Your faith must be moved to a new level in Christ.

HOPE

What is hope? Hope is a desire based on a promise of God. This promise communicates a possibility of God's blessing to the individual and encourages the soul. If one will plant his seed into the soil of the heart and if the soil is kept right, it will bring forth a harvest of faith.

BIBLE HOPE

Bible hope is similar to natural hope, in that it is also a belief in the possible expectation of a desire. The difference is that the foundation for Bible hope is not founded on earthly reason, but rather on the promises given to us in the bible from God.

> Romans 15:4 – "For whatever was written in earlier times were written for our instruction, so that through perseverance and the encouragement of the scriptures we might have hope."

> Ephesians 2:12 – "Remember that you were at that time separate from Christ, excluded from the commonwealth of Israel, and strangers to the covenants of promise, having no hope and without God in the world."

Now, let's define NATURAL HOPE VS. GOD'S PROMISED HOPE

This topic brings me to the remembrance of Abraham and Sarah. When these two were beyond the childbearing years, they could not see their way of having a child. They were beyond hopelessness. But hope is a "just cause" reason for it to happen. Childbearing was not something they could even fathom. Abraham could not depend upon natural hope. Because naturally, it was not going to happen. However, God gave Abraham a promise and that promise was that he was going to have a child with his wife Sarah. On the hope of *that* promise, he was able to have a God Promise Hope. Abraham believed God that He was going to fulfil his promise to him. And in exchange for that belief, the Bible says that "It was credited to him for righteousness." Basically, Abraham was still going to receive his answer. His hope was not in the natural any longer but he was in God's promised hope. In all of this to say, we are to look beyond our natural circumstances. We're not to deny our natural situations and circumstances but we should look beyond them. In Romans 4:17 it states: "Abraham believed God, who gives life to the dead and calls those things that be not as though they were." Hope and faith are not based on a denial of natural conditions. They are based on God's spoken word despite natural conditions. It is a belief that God will change the natural circumstances to fulfill that promise. That promise must be known, received, and believed. And acted upon. This is the walk of faith and this was a complete success.

LOVE

I remember as a child and in my adult life, my mother would always say "love is an action word." She would always tell me "you can say that you love someone, but you have to put it into action." Love is an action word. She has inspired me to love unconditionally and to love in my heartache and pain. Also to love when there was no love that would be returned. So you must act upon the word Love and put it into action.

The Bible says in 1 Corinthians 13: 4-8: "Love is patient and kind. Love does not envy or boast. It is not arrogant or rude. It does not insist on its own way. It is not irritable or resentful. It does not rejoice at wrongdoing but rejoices with the truth. Love bears all things, believes all things, hopes all things and endures all things. Love never ends. As for prophecies, they will pass away; as for tongues, they will cease, as for knowledge, it will pass away."

WHAT DOES THE BIBLE SAY ABOUT LOVE?

"If anyone says, "I love God," and hates his brother, he is a liar, for he who does not love his brother or sister whom he has seen cannot love God whom he has not seen." - 1 John 4:20. For you are not operating in the right love, not God's love. You need to go back and re-evaluate yourself and do a reality check to make sure your heart is pure and righteous.

> "But the fruit of the spirit is love, joy, peace, patience, kindness, goodness, faithfulness, gentleness, self-control, against such things there is no law." - Galatians 5:22

Chapter Five

TRUE FRIENDSHIP

PROVERBS 18:24

One thing I wanted to touch on in this book is "True Friendship." The subject of true friendship has been on my mind lately. So I went to the Bible to find out what God says about friendship. What is true friendship? What does it look like to be a good friend or to experience true friendship with another person? It has been my experience that true friendship is not always obvious. A person you thought was your friend may turn out to be disloyal and those that you thought didn't care as much for you may turn out to be your closest allies. Therefore, the Bible states, it is wise to "try" a friendship to make sure it is true. In Proverbs 27:17 it states, "As iron sharpens iron, so one person sharpens another."

There is a mutual benefit in the rubbing of two blades together, the edges become sharper, making the knives more efficient in their task to cut and slice. I should be able to sharpen a friend's edges, dull areas and she should be able to do the same for me—where we both can build one another up so that the other can become better, wiser and stronger. If you are a true friend you will tell that friend if he or she is in the wrong, you tell him the truth even if it will be hard for him to hear. If you are the friend receiving advice, the Bible says "If you listen in correction, you will grow in understanding" (Proverbs 15:32) Who you take advice from is one of the most important decisions we must make to become a woman of great character and great faith.

Let's see what the Bible says about Friendship from another perspective. It gives a few warnings about friends. It says, a friend who is as close as your own soul has the power to entice you to sin. "And that prophet, or that dreamer of dreams, shall be put to death, because he hath spoken to turn you away from the Lord your God, which brought you out the land of Egypt, and redeemed you out the house of bondage. To thrust thee out of the way which the Lord thy God commanded you to walk in. If thy brother, the son of thy mother, or thy son, or thy daughter, or the wife of thy bosom, or thy friend, which is as thy own soul, entice thee secretly, saying, Let us go and serve other gods, which thou hast not known, thou, nor thy fathers; Namely, of the gods of the people which are round about you, nigh unto thee, or far off from thee, from the one end of the earth even unto the other end of the earth" (Deuteronomy 13:5-7 KJV)

In Psalm 55:12-14 it says, "For it was not an enemy that reproached me; then I could have borne it: neither was it he that did magnify himself against me; then I would have hid myself from him: But it was thou, a man mine equal, my guide and mine acquaintance. We took sweet counsel together, and walked unto the house of God in company."

If you're smart, you will accept the advice from the wise friend and reject the advice that will lead your heart astray from doing the will of God. Of course we should always first turn to God for advice and listen to the Holy Spirit for direction. However, the Bible says that when we are seeking guidance from a friend, the godly will give us good advice. Personally, after years of confiding in the wrong people, I have now learned to tame my tongue and only share my private matters with the people who will offer me heavenly advice and who I know I can trust.

Our goal as women of faith is to build our Christ-like character, and confiding in a friend who will provide heavenly wisdom, is one way to grow in your spiritual maturity. Choosing to confide in the wrong friends will only add wood to the 'fires' in your life. This will always result in a loss of your heart to resemble the aftermath of a massive forest fire.

A friend who turns against you is unbearable, much worse than an enemy. And when it comes to true friendship, the Bible implies that larger numbers does not always mean safety. So just because you have many friends does not mean they are all faithful and true. In Proverbs 18:24 NKJV it says, "a man *who* has friends must himself be friendly, but there is a friend *who* sticks closer than a brother."

Here are some questions to ask yourself:

1. Do I know the people I need to not share my problems with?
2. Who will I go to for advice from now on?
3. Who will I share my worries with?
4. Am I a friend that offers heavenly wisdom, good advice to my friends?
5. How well do I take correction from a true friend?
6. Do I know the difference between good advice and foolish advice?

I pray you will be reminded to share your struggles and conflicts with friends who you can trust in to give you words of wisdom which are from the fountain of life. Instead of going to one another with issues to 'vent' about, why not approach your trusted friend by saying, "I am going through something right now and I need your advice." Not only will this slap the spirit of gossip in the face, but that friend will be prepared to give you the right advice as opposed to just listening to you 'vent'. If you aren't surrounded by many 'godly' friends who you can talk to or ask for advice, why not connect with another woman of faith on Facebook or via email?

TRUE FRIENDSHIP: WHAT IS IT?

A true friend is a very rare thing, but when it is proven it is something to treasure and keep safe by all means possible. So what are the hallmarks of a true friendship? How do you really know when a friend really loves you? There are three verses I want to focus on to illustrate true friendship. The first one is Proverbs 17:17: "A friend loves at all times and a brother is born for adversity."

TRUE FRIENDSHIP: THE WOUNDS OF A FRIENDSHIP

The second verse is Proverbs 27: 6 NKJV: "Faithful are the wounds of a friend, But the kisses of an enemy are deceitful." It is common for a true friendship to be marked by wounds. As we live life together, situations arise where true friendship must express itself by one friend wounding another, or being willing to sustain wounds.

A true friend of an addict, for example, may endure his friend's abuse in order to intervene on his friend's behalf. We may also have to hurt a friend (or allow ourselves to be hurt) in order to do what is most loving and right for that person.

TRUE FRIENDSHIP: THE TRUEST FRIEND

The third verse is John 15: 13 NKJV: "Greater love has no one than this, than to lay down one's life for his friends."

The greatest example of this is the action God takes in our lives. True friendship means laying down your very life, if necessary, for the good of a friend. I don't know a person that would exemplify this. But this is the way God loves us. He gives us what is good for us, not what we want or deserve. Happily, there are times when they do not coincide and when our foolish hearts long for what will ultimately make us miserable, God is willing to break our hearts to keep us from that misery. Remember, the heart of God is tender. When our hearts are broken, he feels it as well. But he is willing to endure with us; that is true friendship.

PERSONAL EXPERIENCE OF TRUE FRIENDSHIP

I have to be honest, in my forty-nine years, I cannot recall or name on one hand the amount of true friends that I've had in my life. Although, I have never been the kind of woman who felt that she had to have a lot of girlfriends either. The ones I have encountered I would most certainly call them "associates" or "acquaintances." They have never shown me nor demonstrated towards me that they would have my back or would lay down their lives for me.

Every time we would talk on the phone or visit with one another, they never really had an inspiring word for me. They never edified nor encouraged me in any area of my life or what I was dealing with at that time in my life. It was always some kind of drama that was going on in *their* life. Never did they ask me how my life was going or how I was doing. They were connected to me for only one reason and that was to get what they could out of me. I truly felt I was a friend with benefits for them.

I truly believe that there are people in our lives who are there just to get what they want from you. Their motives are to boost themselves through you because they see something in you that attracts them. They feel or think that it can get them to a higher place of living. But, you only go higher in your living when you go higher in your giving. However, what they fail to realize is that there is only one of you. Whatever they are trying to get or do through you simply will not work. What's in their hands won't do the same thing when it's in your hands. Basically, what I'm saying is that God has ordained you and ordered "your" steps specifically for you. What your hands touch will not come out or flourish the same way when their hands touch it. God has equipped you for the task, the assignment and the job, not them. *Your* results will be *your* results. Have you ever heard the song? "What God has for me, it is for me."

Going on to say, having friends is fine. There is nothing wrong with a woman having friends. But a friendship has to be tested in order for a person to call them a friend. Having a good friendship is not always equal to having a good time. They come with challenging times, bad times, and even hardships. Something worth having is always worth working towards and is never easy. What's easy for you, may not always be good for you or worth having. The harder you had to obtain things, are usually worth keeping.

This analogy brings me to one of my true friends in which I only had one of. We met in the early 1970's. I had to be about five or six years old and she was about four. I can remember our first memorable moments. Our families were close and we were considered to be close family friends. My family moved away to another city in 1976 which saddened my siblings and me. But in 1978 when I was twelve years old, we returned back to the city where we had moved from. We couldn't have been happier!

She and I have been inseparable ever since. We have gone through good times and bad. We've worked through them, stumbled, fell, got back up, went in different directions in life, have had children, gotten married, gotten divorced, had college experiences, bought and built homes, sold homes, have had challenges with our children, moved to different states and through it all we are still friends. She has been the only one who stuck it out with me. No matter what, we take our friendship seriously. She's probably the only one I can talk with just about anything and I've confided in her almost about everything! I don't think she's held her tongue back either in regards to me.

But four years ago, not only did our friendship reach another level but it also went to the next plateau. Our relationship became even more meaningful because it was related to the Lord. We are both saved and have a relationship with God which makes mine and her relationship with each other better and stronger. Now, God is our connecting point. You friendship may reach another level with being friends with that special someone, a good girlfriend, or what we call them today, "BFF's" (A Best Friend Forever) that's all good and dandy, but when the friendship relates to our Heavenly Father, it has reached that next plateau. There's a different kind of feeling you acquire when you can have a girlfriend that prays in the morning before she starts her day, that meditates on the things of God, pray and acknowledges God. Being someone's BFF doesn't compare to a GFF! (A God Friend Forever)

True friends don't wake up on the same side of the bed every day and doesn't have to talk every day on the phone. Talking on the phone every day can and just may lead into gossip. She knows her place in the friendship and will uphold it without insecurities. When you have children, a full-time job, activities going on, in ministry, responsibilities, and commitments there's no time to play house with friends, not every day. You can catch up with what's going on with one another and even plan a Saturday just for the two of you; there's absolutely nothing wrong with that. But as you get older, you should become wiser too. Know where your priorities lie. Personally, I am about my Father's business, so I rarely talk to girlfriends on a daily basis. I really don't have anything to say in that fashion to a woman every day. Now there's nothing wrong with contacting your girlfriend on the phone and having girl talk, but my time must go elsewhere to be successful. Successful women think differently. Doing too much of one thing or keeping company of someone or something too much is not always good for you. What you do too much of or be around too often causes you to become as such. You still must protect your spirit.

If at all possible, surround yourself with people, women specifically, who are doing greater things than you are. Be around people doing positive things. Meaning for the community or speaking at functions or someone who is going in the right direction in their life. Hang around women who are smarter than you; they're the ones that can help you reach your goals. You may not know exactly how to get there, the right avenues or roads to take but they do. Their knowledge can entice your search for knowledge. Their lead can help lead you further. Just pay attention, take notes and following their lead can take you to greater grounds and higher heights. A real friend will lead you into the right direction, guide you, and give you the necessary tools to help you succeed. Yes, a real friend will do that for you.

THE BREAKDOWN

I searched the word "friend" from the Merriam-Webster Dictionary and it declares:

A person who you like and enjoy BEING with: a person who helps or supports something (such as a cause or charity). I would like to point out two keywords in this definition that I feel are important. The word "Helps" and "Supports." Being a friend, helping and supporting them are key factors in a true friendship. In my personal life I have experienced people who I have considered to be their friend because I have helped and supported them. But not once have they ever offered or extended any assistance or a helping hand to help or support me in my time of need or hardship. At times, people seem to want to be a friend to you or want to call you their friend but they don't know how or don't know what it takes to achieve that status for them to be that for you.

Chapter Six

MARRIAGE, RELATIONSHIPS, & SINGLENESS

MARRIAGE

GENESIS 2:24: "THEREFORE SHALL A MAN LEAVE HIS FATHER AND HIS MOTHER, AND SHALL CLEAVE UNTO HIS WIFE: AND THEY SHALL BE ONE FLESH."

Marriage is a job just as much as when you go to work every day; we punch a time clock eight, ten, and sometimes twelve plus hours a day. We may work a nine-to-five shift, report to our assignments or to our boss to begin a day's work. That's why it is said you have to work on your marriage every day! However, in marriage the job is no longer limited to a nine-to-five time-frame. It's a twenty-four-hour and seven-day-a-week job. Marriages have no weekends off; you can't choose your own shift and it is mandatory to be in attendance seven days a week, instead of the five-day work week and three hundred sixty-five days a year. It doesn't require approval from any supervisor for the overtime to be put in. Husbands and wives are their own supervisors. So, in all of this, know that marriage is and can be a beautiful match made in heaven. Know that wives and husbands are "Better, Together." I pray the scripture below will bless you:

In Ephesians 5:22-25 it states, 22 "Wives, submit yourselves to your own husbands as you do to the Lord. 23 For the husband is the head of the wife as Christ is the head of the church, his body, of which he is the Savior. 24 Now as the church submits to Christ, so also wives should submit to their husbands in everything.

25 Husbands, love your wives, just as Christ loves the church and gave himself up for her."

IS GOD INVITED? GOD'S INVITATION
TO YOUR MARRIAGE

Being a divorced woman, I can't tell you in this book how to keep your marriage strong and forever lasting. However, I can tell you how to not let it end in divorce. I truly don't understand how a marriage can survive without God being a participant. Inviting God into your marriage would be an absolute important invitation so that He can be the coordinator and orchestrator of your marriage.

The husband and wife should be in the word of God. If you are, awesome! If you're not, ouch! The Bible speaks about the husband and wife being unequal and the warning signs of you being so. If the two parties are unequally yoked, there can be and will always be a strain on your marriage. Do not be yoked together with unbelievers. For what do righteousness and wickedness have in common? In my past relationships, it did not take a rocket scientist to figure this one out. I, the church girl and he, well just a 360 degree opposite— it was definitely a case of opposites attract! I truly thank God now that His hand did not bless those relationships. God was never going to simply because He does not bless sin. Thank you Lord God. Being unequally yoked can add more strain on top of the marriage or relationship itself which can lead to more stress than you bargained for. In 2 Corinthians 6:14 it says "Be ye not unequally yoked with unbelievers together with righteousness with unrighteousness? And what communion hath light with darkness."

WARNING: Don't become partners with those who reject God. How can you make a partnership with right and wrong? That's not partnership; that's war. Is light best friends with dark? Does Christ go strolling with the Devil? The verse in 2 Corinthians 6:14 it doesn't say, "Do not be unequally yoked unless you think the person will change" It says, "Do not be yoked together with unbelievers" He or she may be a Christian, know of God, acknowledge him, accepted him and even been baptized in God. But they are not real and true believers. They are far from believing the things of God and what He is and can do. They have no real and true relationship with God and certainly are not a believer of the faith. There's a difference.

There is no such thing as a perfect marriage. It's going to take both of you to strive, work, put forth real effort and love unconditionally to make that M-Word work. Here me out, you have two different lives and lifestyles that you're trying to bridge together to become as one. Mind you, there's two different backgrounds, upbringings, personalities, family lifestyles, habits, likes, dislikes, mindsets, goal sets, different credit scores, house cleaning techniques, body cleanliness, different communication skills, handling your finances on different levels, and the list goes on. Now tell me, who can master this without conflict? I haven't found one yet. When you do, let me know. Although there are many different characteristics to work on and smooth out, it can be done and possible to succeed.

WHO'S THE KEYNOTE SPEAKER?

Will your marriage survive without God being the Keynote Speaker? He is the key that can and will unlock the door to a successful marriage. Secondly, be sensitive to the voice of God so that you can be obedient and take notes from him. Listen to God so you can stay on the right path as it relates to your marriage. Thirdly, allow God's spirit to speak to you and allow Him to be the speaker for you. I have always told women, when they're in a relationship, it is so important to have time alone with God. Go into your prayer closet, find a space, an area of your home and have quiet time or "me" time with God. Ask God to lead you in your relationship; ask Him for insight of where the relationship is going. He will give you what to say and how to say to your mate. Often times, we are the talkers in the relationship and we never know when to tune it down and yes, turn down too!

We always want to give the man a piece of our minds or tell them what we think. But if you don't say anything and keep quiet, God will begin to speak into your spirit and lead you of what and how to speak to him, but most importantly when to say it too. Let him dwell there in the midst of your mind. So giving your mate a piece of your mind will get you nowhere. But if you consult God first, and speak to your mate just as God directed you to do, your relationship will soar in more ways and he will embrace the conversation better than before. Keep God as the third party and allow Him to be the leader. Allow Him to lead and guide you; He won't steer you wrong or take you down the wrong road. He'll even be the GPS and take you in the right direction without any wrong turns.

THE WEAKER VESSEL VS. THE STRONGER VESSEL

God made the man to be the leader and to lead. He made man to be the stronger vessel and the woman the weaker vessel. When God created man, there were certain things that he implanted into him that were intentionally and diligently designed on how a man should be as it relates to his manhood. With what the man is supposed to do in critical thinking situations, emergencies and an unexpected crisis. There are things that a man should automatically have instilled in him in terms of what to do and how to do in the form of being a husband. Understandably so, there are times when and where the man perhaps did not have a father figure or a male role model in their lives when they were growing up, but there's an answer to that scenario and here it is! If he turns to God in prayer and supplication, yearns for the right way in doing what his God-given role is, God will teach him through the word of God how to be the best husband for his spouse, tailor made just for her. It is ok to trust in the Lord with all your heart and lean not on your own understanding (Proverbs 3:5) A man cannot truly lead and be the leader of his home when he is not being led by God. He must pray, listen to God, humble himself, and be sensitive to the voice of God.

There are also certain elements that God placed in the woman that he did not place in man. As God would have it in which he designed it, for the woman to be the weaker vessel in the marriage, she can only endure so much. Endure meaning handle, take on, uphold, and do within her inner womanly power. Women have a nurturing spirit. We are easy to nurture and but not so easy to understand. Our spirits nurture automatically. We have certain techniques built in us that we use to implement care. Whether it's in taking care of business, parenting, cooking, and even in the simplicity of folding up towels and sheets. We have a certain way of doing things differently than how a man would.

On the other hand, men are the total opposite. Just observe the man in your life sometimes while he's doing daily activities and see the contrast of how he handles them as opposed to how you would handle them as a woman. So, if your husband or man just don't do as quite good of a job as you do in washing dishes, just pat him on the back, and give him a kiss on the cheek and tell him thank you. In 1 Peter 3:7 it speaks about the woman being the weaker vessel: "In the same way, your husbands must give honor to your wives, and treat your wife with understanding as you live together. She may be weaker than you, but she is your equal partner in God's gift of new life. Treat her as you should so your prayers will not be hindered."

IS MARRIAGE FOR YOU?

In my personal journey as a married woman, I did not follow God's commandments. I tried to be the leader, the head; this role was not meant for a woman to take on. I didn't stay in my lane. I went into his and then he became bombarded by my traffic, too many green lights of the presence as his wife. I ran stop signs, went thru red lights, didn't slow down for the yellow flashing lights and ignored all the yield signs. I was still consumed with a lot of my single ways that I brought into my marriage. I later found out the hard way because when you're single, things are much different than when you're married. Being a non-married person, you operate differently and your mindset isn't operating in a state of a partnership and unity. I had a one-track mind. One in which I became off track while being a married woman. I was not fully engaged as a wife in my marriage, meaning I was committed and loyal to him physically, spiritually, and emotionally but I was distant and a million miles away, mentally.

I look back now and wonder if I was the cause of him not doing what he desired to do for me or needed to do in the marriage. I was very strong willed, empowered, and strong minded. I moved on my own time and in my own thinking. One thing I've learned is that a woman should go to God in prayer regarding her marriage and relationships. Ask God to lead you in that marriage or relationship and to be the wife or woman that He has ordained you to be. If you don't know where to start or what to ask God for you can surely start off by going to Him and specifically saying, "I don't know Lord where to start or how to pray" even if you don't know what scriptures to seek. Ask for knowledge to lead you to the right scripture for that exact time of your need. Cry out to God and He will make all the impossibles possible. He will make it just right for you and give you exactly what you need. Whether you're married or not, a Christian woman needs to know how to operate in the spirit realm and not of the flesh in the time of her need. That flesh will not get you what you need when you're in a crisis and you need God to show up now!

YOUR DIFFERENCES MAKES THE DIFFERENCE

Men and women have such a difference in our makeup and in our being, even when it comes to our thought processes. Men and women think very differently from each other, but it doesn't mean you have to get a divorce just because the two of you have different thought processes. It's really okay. We're supposed to think different because that's the way God made us. It is the life that we live that makes the difference. I think it's awesome for two people in a relationship to come together and sort out their differences. They can still come to common ground and say, we are better, together. In that, they can move forward, have their differences and be different in God. Wow, now that's pretty awesome!

STIMULATE THE MIND

They say that a mind is a terrible thing to waste. I truly believe that because we as women don't believe in wasting anything, especially our minds. When God made the mind, I wonder what He had in mind, at least for the woman. Most women like to be challenged, we can articulate and figure out something keen by what someone says to us and we can usually process it pretty quickly. Our minds may be sharp as a whip, but we also like for our minds to be stimulated by the opposite sex. Women also are stimulated by what and how she feels. Our minds are like keepsake tools. Not necessarily physically or sexually, but we as women are turned on quickly even just by how a man looks in a pair of nice slacks or the smell of his cologne. We can also get turned off even quicker, just by the first three minutes of his conversation or if his shoes are dirty. We get to thinking quickly, with that mind again—how that man would look next to us with those nice slacks on or thinking how well that cologne smelled. That's when we have to put our minds under subjection and keep the spirit over the mind. Not the mind over the spirit. If the mind is over the spirit there will be a disorder. The spirit must be over our mind in order for God to fulfill our destiny.

Women are very sensitive and we are emotional creatures too, period. Especially when we get into our feelings, where and how we want to be touched and the way we're spoken to. We even cry more easily. Our hearts are more tender and our feelings get hurt faster also. There's a scriptures that reminds me of how we as women are emotional creatures and what we will do to protect our hearts. In Proverbs 4:23 it says "Keep your heart with diligence, for out of it are the issues of life." This passage is saying, guard and protect your heart because you never know what it may have to endure. However, when it comes to us forgetting about something, a situation or something a man said to us or how he treated us ten years ago, forget it! We have not perfected that word "Forget" yet! We will not and do not forget easily. We will not forgive him so easily either. Unfortunately, we will hold onto that thing forever and keep it at his remembrance until the day of Pentecost, if we could.

We won't let go of the hurt and we'll even throw it in his face or bring it back up to his attention for years or years later. This is because we are very sensitive when it comes to our hearts and we are emotional alarm clocks as well.

RELATIONSHIPS

When dating or in a relationship, there should be a certain compatibility level that two individuals should have while courting, especially in the spirit realm. You must be yoked for one another and make sure at some capacity you are not only physically attracted to your potential mate but spiritually attracted to him also. That is a must. Even if he or she is not at the same spiritual level as you are, they should be intelligent enough to be able to relate to you in some of the same areas in the spirit realm. Whether these areas are having and acting upon Godly principles, having the fear of God in them, church attendance and how often they go, being spiritually minded, setting goals, have similar mindsets, being family-oriented, career path set and how long you should date before getting married. As Christians, the expectation level the two should have of one another should reach far beyond than just dating. Dating just to be dating for pleasure or for fun is a waste of time. There should be a purpose in dating and that purpose should be discussed right at the top of you coming together.

If the two parties are not on the same level of expectation of where the relationship should go and in the length of time, then it's probably best that you cut it off right then. I say this because you just don't want to waste your time. When God could have someone waiting to approach you and sweep you off your feet, court you the right way and be the man that God has for you. You won't have to look for him, because he surely will find you. Yes, he will! In Proverbs 18:22 it states "He who finds a wife finds a good thing, and obtains favor from the Lord." This particular scripture is saying that you can go ahead about your life, minding your business, your daily doings, activities, etc. Because when the Lord is done preparing, molding and shaping him for you, he *will* be *just* for you. Make sure you ask God exactly the things you desire in a mate. God likes for us to come to Him in that way. Yes, you should go to God in detail entailing and asking God specifically what you desire in a husband. And you're Father will deliver just as you asked. - In James 4:2 it says "We have not because we ask not." We should ask for the things we want, even our desires in a mate.

Most importantly, religious beliefs and spiritual backgrounds must be key factors in your relationship. I would never again consider dating any man that I was not spiritually connected too. That's one thing that you don't go to the bargaining table with. Count that a deal breaker and count it out! He would definitely have to have some kind of connection to God and must be a believer.

His level of spirituality would have to well exceed that of the average Christian man. Being the woman that I am and the caliber of which I carry, I could not settle for a potential mate that would not be willing to stand with me, uphold me, or support me on the levels that I am destined to reach. Being a Christian would absolutely have to be a prerequisite for anyone you date. Anyone you meet that says they are not a Christian should be a red flag and you should run fast in the opposite direction. There should be no discussion or compromising of why he or she must be a Christian to date you. There are just certain standards that you must hold in high regard and your beliefs you must place even higher.

Not only does the person you decide to date need to be a Christian or saved but they need to be spiritually seasoned enough to be able to relate to you. As beautiful as he or she may be, it's going to take more than physical attributes to help get you through some things or the tough times that are going to come. It's going to take some listening, understanding, encouraging, some tears, some real hanging in there, some holding on and some real knee bending praying to get the two of you through some hardships, temptations, tests, trials and the schemes of the enemy.

SINGLENESS

DEFENSE

Are you a single Christian woman or man and you have come to the determination that you are ready to start dating? Well, there are some qualifications you need to check out and see if they're going to qualify to date you. Dating in the Christian world is serious business. There's no time for watch and see. But watch and pray. You'll know when you're ready to start dating and know when you're not ready. As for myself, being a single Christian woman, whenever I would meet a certain man, I knew after the first two or three minutes of our conversation if he was qualified to get to know me better or date me.

As women, we should have our invisible detectors ready to detect the dialect of what the man is speaking to her. In those two or three minutes of conversing with him, she should be able to know a little about him. His motives, character and intentions should well be clear to her. If your spiritual eyes detect something that your natural eyes can't or if the spirit over your mind, is unclear about this prospect. There's no need to exchange phone numbers or setup any future dates. A woman of God must remember that she is rare, radiant, and should be spoken to and treated like royalty.

If he does not make eye contact with you while talking to you, he's really not into you. If he's moving his body around and arms in swinging motions, he doesn't have your best interest at heart. If he's talking with his hands during the whole time you're in his presence upon meeting, he's just simply not the one. Being that you're a saved woman, he should notice immediately that there is something different about you from the rest. He should see a glow, something in you that shows a difference from the rest. The way that you speak, the way you respond just in simple gestures even by how you get in your car. Trust me, men notice everything because they're very visual. And if his tenacity is on point, he'll know you're not just a blow. Men treat women on a higher plateau when he sees and knows she is about her business and she is not to be gamed with nor is she a push over. He will speak to her differently accordingly to how she's dressed. If I can give women any advice right now, I'd say "Dress How You Want to be Addressed." Men, there's a flip side to this also. There is a respect level that a man receives and achieves from a woman when she sees he's taking care of business with her too.

PAST TENSE

It is critical and crucial for the Christian woman to know the past of a potential mate. His past will truly make a difference on how it will affect your life and it will be with him in the present and future. You need to be aware of what you're getting yourself into. You should know if he was raised in the church or if his parents even went to church. More so if his parents loved the Lord. Where they churchgoers or members of a church? Were his parents involved in any ministries? How was he raised? Was he raised in a two-parent or single-parent household? What are his morals and values, his cleanliness and his showering and bathing patterns? Yes, how nasty or clean he is!

You must know these things before you decide to get involved with a certain individual. These can affect your home life as well as your mental and spiritual life. You want everything out in the open on the table before you proceed with the relationship. This is something we don't do. We wait until we're involved in the relationship for six months then we find these things out after we get emotionally attached, and find these things out later. Now, you have problems. So it is better to have an attraction and not go forth in the relationship rather than to go forth in the relationship and have friction and distraction later.

OFFENSE

The Christian single woman must use her discernment intellect and supernatural power to know what is off limits to her and for her—DEAL BREAKERS. I know we are women first and we were all born into sin and we all are sinners saved by grace. But this doesn't mean we have to accept or tolerate just anything or anyone to be in our presence or entertain foolishness. We must know when and when not to move and go forth. If you are in the word of God daily, fasting and praying, then the spirit of the Lord should lead and guide you down the path of righteousness. Your anointing should be so ever-present that no man can just approach you; the anointing won't let him. God just won't allow it. God protects what's His. If this man isn't in his lead role or trying to go to church with you on Sunday mornings nor if he's not accompany you to Bible Study sometimes and support you with church functions, etc. Now that is a total deal breaker. No questions, no comment. Period.

SINGLE PEOPLE

Single people should first date themselves. If you don't enjoy being in your own company, perhaps your date won't either. If you find yourself being boring, most likely, he or she will be bored with you too. You must first have a life strategy as a single person to set yourself up for your own goals, life plans and self-awareness. Self-Esteem is very important if you're looking to date. Make sure you build your esteem on you whether you find somebody or not.

COMMUNICATION

I am the kind of person who enjoys communicating. But not only do I like to communicate, I like to communicate in different ways and on different levels. Your mate must be compatible to your communication level. He must communicate with you to the point that it changes the dialogue you two started off with and will come onto another level of understanding of one another. As I like to say, "Make love to my mind." He must be attracted to my mental state without the physical aspect. There should something else there that will hold your mate to you besides a physical attraction. There are other attractions such as, spiritual beauty, mental, and emotionally tied. So we must be able to connect and be compatible in more ways than the physical. I thought about what happens when the physical part has a little wear and tear to it and you're just not into the physical that day. You're in need of something else to mentally and spiritually stimulate you. Then what? So, there has to be something more that's going to keep you there, involved and attracted to your mate and keep you there in their corner at all times.

You're going to have to know how to communicate with your spouse and also when to communicate with them. In Matthew 11:29, the Bible says "Take my yoke upon you and learn from me." What God continues to say is "Come to him, learn his ways, learn how to trust him, learn his inside out." So I say to you, learn your mate. Know when to go to him and discuss things. Know when and how to approach him and know when to let him be alone.

When he walks through the door from work or when you know he's had a hard day, that is not the time to come right at him with things that can be discussed later. Instead, when your husband walks through the door, give him a hug or a kiss and let tell him how much you missed him. Or, when your "husband" is taking off his work clothes, just give him a soft kiss on his forehead and tell him everything he may have weighing on his mind is going to be okay even if you don't see a foreseeable situation or if he doesn't insinuate there's a problem. Men love reassurance. They like to be reassured that their family, job and home life is secure by none other than his partner for life, his wife. Communication is such an important element in relationships. It's the tone of how you set the communication to be. Remember, it's not what you say to a person, but *how* you say it that makes the difference. Communicating can keep the enemy out of your relationship. It keeps the spirit of silence away and it keeps the spirit of doubt away as well. Remember, you want your mate to stimulate your mind. Some men aren't as good of communicators as others. I mean, they just will not talk. Believe me, I had one before and I'll leave that one right there. As I stated before, I particularly am the communicative type. With an individual failing to reciprocate this back to you, your relationship may struggle and will stay on the verge of hardship.

Side note: You cannot allow anyone to hinder you from communicating because they don't know how to or do not have a desire to.

The meaning of "Communicate" is: To share or exchange information, news or ideas to someone by speaking, writing, moving your hands, etc. To get someone to understand your thoughts or feelings.

Chapter Seven

A CLASS ACT

MATTHEW 7: 1-5

A classy woman can be seen from afar. She can also be spotted miles away. Her peers will notice the character she carries. But a Christian and classy woman comes second to none. When you put these two together, all eyes are on her. She can make her entrance and presence known even without announcing herself. Her friends, family, associates, peers, and her doubters will take notice of a difference in and about her.

It takes a special kind of woman to operate in who she is. There has to be a special calling on a Christian woman's life to be set apart from the rest of her counterparts. Being set apart will come with some mistreatments, gossip, and harmful attacks against her. As I spoke about this in a previous text it may come at a cost when the anointing is on her life. I am a living witness that God's anointing shall over reign anything that tries to come her way.

A CLASS ACT entails that you are a classy woman, which came by a work in progress. I'd say, it took a whole lot of "Acting" in order to get it right. You acted one way one year, then another way the next year until you stumbled on God's way which was the final and right way. You got right with Your Lord, then you "Acted" upon cleansing yourself with righteousness. After all these "Actions" have taken place now, you've become A Class Act. I named the last chapter this because after all that we as women have gone through in life, all that we have endured and all that shall yet come our way, we are Obstacle Overcomers in A Class Act.

Believe me, it took an enormous amount of time for God to transform my life, my ways, my heart, and me as a woman. So I am not to be misunderstood, I was not always the woman you see now. Women especially seem to always judge other women by the way they look, talk, walk, the way they carry themselves and even by their careers. Not fully understanding how she got to where she is in life or in which she came. What she had to go through, the hurdles, the steps, stumbles, falls and road blocks she had to tumble through. I say to you, Overcomer, until you're ready and willing to face the fire and literally go through everything that the one you're judging or looking at in a dismantling way, don't judge her. You don't know what she had to go through or endure. Life is very real and it can be told best by you, The Overcomer! Again, God chooses certain people to face certain situations so they can best tell of His goodness.

I know He chose me in July 1999 when I became a burn victim. I will never forget that day because I faced the fire literally and how the electricity went through my body. But God chose to keep me here; He sustained me and healed my body. That is why I give Him praise and honor the way that I do. Very few know of my past and what I went through. But now that the world knows and I pray that it will help someone, even just one. The dead and burnt skin, my flesh that had to be pulled off my body to decrease the risk of infection and how I watch the nurses peel my skin off like I was a rag doll, it came off just like paper. How I had to soak in ice cold water for hours at a time, how I could not use that part of the body sufficiently for nearly two years. I went onto having physical therapy once a week for six months, how I had to be measured for pressure garments just so the garments would fit tight and snugged to my skin to smoothen the skin to decrease scar tissue. The skin graft that draped my body with medical aluminum foil tightly pulled away my flesh. How my two young sons had to prepare my meals for me, feed me, bathe me, brush my hair, and rub my body with soothing cream. All at the tender ages of six and twelve. I was helpless, but we knew where our help came from.

So women, before it enters into your mind and vocabulary, think before you judge. We are so quick to assume or reject someone else before we can get to know her. That "her" may be able to help you in areas of your life where you are struggling or can't see your way through.

Today we are so critical of one another. We forsake and discouraged someone without us really knowing that we are actually doing it. Growing up, we may have heard our parents or adults say a curse word and perhaps it made the person that they were speaking to feel dismayed. Often times, we unknowingly hold onto those spirits from our youth and adolescence and take them with us into our adulthood. Then, when we have a confrontation or misunderstanding with someone we automatically blur out negative words towards them. We say hurtful things to them without knowing that we are really doing more harm to them than good. But you can fight the harm off of you if you choose to. In families today, mothers are against daughters, daughters against mothers, fathers are against sons, sons against fathers, sisters against sisters, brothers against brothers, uncles against nephews and nieces against aunts. They have stopped speaking to one another.

When people such as family, friends, associates have all stop socializing and talking to you, count it all joy. It's working altogether for your good. You may have to be lied on, talked about, cheated, called the black sheep of the family, but nevertheless, defeated. You may not know why or fully understand why this is happening but know that God is going bring you out of it all.

After you endure all the judging and mistreatment from these people and your enemies, God will say when enough is enough. When He does it will be His time to be glorified through you and bring you out of your storm, your heartache and pain. I don't care what it seems like or what it looks like. Just stand! You may feel at times you've been knocked down but when you get up and when God brings you out the world will know it. In 2 Corinthians 4:8,9 it states: We are troubled on every side, yet not distressed;

we are perplexed, but not despair; Persecuted, but not forsaken; cast down, but not destroyed;

PRESENTATION

How you present yourself to others is a vital part of your life. People are always watching. It's like the world is keeping track of you, your every move and what you say. Did you know that there are people waiting for you to say to the wrong thing? They will actually sit before you be in the midst of your company, smile in your face, and then run back and gossip about you of what you said, only difference is they'll twist it around and spit it out from the gates of hell and by time it gets back to you, it's nothing like the you said or the original statement. There are ways of making sure you present yourself with honor and dignity. Here are some of those reasons why: You never know who's watching you. You can be watched from near or far. People watch everything you do. They say the eye is the naked truth. So wherever you are, you always want to speak intelligently and intellectually. Speak clearly and articulately so no words are misinterpreted, misunderstood, misplaced, and misguided. That way no one will be able to tell you what you said or didn't say. So always think first before you speak. There are people that are jealous of you, mad at you because you conduct and carry yourself a certain way.

You want to always dress appropriately and conservatively. Most of the time, men can get by dressing the way they want, but this is especially for women. You want to maintain a clean and professional look. Walk with confidence, not arrogance. Be vigilant and you don't want to be vulgar.

You always want to be mindful that everyone is not going to like you, salute you, or promote you. They're are jealous people! Some call them haters, they're around you too. They may smile at you but really aren't for you. The devil has assigned certain people to attack you, talk about you, belittle you and persecute you. Satan has his angels also and they are out in the world to come against anything positive you do. So don't be surprised when you hear that someone has said something untrue about you. Ultimately, it's to tear down the Kingdom of God because the devil is mad right now at everyone. However, God's Kingdom will always stand and rise to the top. So as I end this segment and say to you, KEEP YOUR CHRISTIANITY, CLASS, AND CHARACTER ALL INTACT.

DRESS HOW YOU WANT TO BE ADDRESSED

Dress with finesse. It is how a woman wears her clothes that will and can speak volume. It will define her personality, her wit, and believe it or not, her reputation. It will tell you how she carries herself. Last but not least, it will signify who will approach her. A woman with class should dress how she wants to be addressed. If you dress with class, tasteful and intact, then that says you demand respect. But if you dress promiscuously, with a lot of skin showing, cleavage and body parts hanging out, you'll attract exactly what is being sought. Because people will see you how you see yourself, especially men.

Your clothes should fit tastefully because your clothes say a lot about your character. It's not only what you wear but how you wear them. Your clothes should not look snug or tight fitting to your body. A woman who dresses with finesse dresses carefully but not carefree. Her clothes should be comfortable fitting. Instead of her looking good in her clothes, the clothes should look good on her.

Although you may be a great match for someone, your clothes don't have to match to a tee. So since the clothes you wear already have been designed, you can definitely be the designee of them. Allow me to give you a quick clothing course! Your style, taste, and niche can be found in your pile of pitch. Toss it up a little bit, the same blue in your blouse doesn't have match the blue in your pants. Always try your clothing on before you actually walk out the house. Do a fit test. See how your attire looks in the mirror to you before you appear in public. If something catches you off course in the mirror, then most likely you are not going to want to be seen out public in them. If you have one, your conscious should let you know.

I know nowadays women like to wear a certain style of clothing for them to be an eye catcher to the opposite sex. She will tend to wear something to catch a man's eye or attention. But ladies allow me to share this with you. A quality man will only seek a quality woman. A real man would not make you his wife. Wearing promiscuous clothing will only make you temporarily to him. Although men may seem to show that they like it. Showing any part of your body is really a turnoff to men. You are to keep your body covered and only for your husband to see, as you may have noticed I said, "husband" not a man. Because intimacy was designed for husband and wife, not for man and woman. It doesn't matter if he's a Christian man or not; a man is a man. Yes, men are stimulated by what they see. Remember, they always like what they see, because they are very visual. But, if that man has any quality about himself, he's not going to take you seriously or date you in a serious manner, let alone be his wife.

FASHIONABLE AND FIERCE

I believe the word "Fashion" seems to always catch a woman's attention. It should also catch her spirit. I know that we love to be fashionable and keep up with the fashion trends of the world today. But remember, we are in the world and not of the world. There are so many catchy clothes, sapphire shoes, sassy sandals, tamed tops, perfecting pumps, sensational skirts, and cliché clothes. But it all depends on who's wearing the clothes that makes it that way. Dressing 'fierce' is one my many favorite things to do. When you dress fierce, you show or kick off a different style of technique that you have with yourself and in your clothes. You know how to set off your clothes just by how you wear them. Your clothes should flow with your personality and your character.

FASHION - Is a popular style or practice, especially in clothing, footwear, accessories, makeup, body or furniture. Fashion is a distinctive and often habitual trend in the style in which a person dresses. It is the prevailing styles in behavior and the newest creations of textile designers.

DRESS - When I searched the word dress it had different meanings, translations, word origins and definitions. But the one that made an impression upon me stated:

Dress - verb: Put on one's clothes

I'm touching on this subject to share a few pointers, suggestions, and spiritual advice as it relates to how women should dress. How she presents herself will make an impression on others. Because we only get one time to make a first impression, right? Whether it be in the workplace, at church, at a restaurant, at an engagement, a business meeting or if you're just running errands. You never know who you'll run into when you're out and about. It could be the opportunity of your life. So, it is always key to present yourself professionally, intellectually and respectfully.

WALK IN CONFIDENCE

Confidence is generally described as a state of being certain, either that a hypothesis or prediction is correct or that a chosen course of action is the best or most effective. Self-confidence is having confidence in oneself. Self-confidence is not a static quality; rather, it's a mindset that takes effort to maintain when the going gets rough. It must be learned, practiced and mastered just like any other skill. But once you master it, you will be changed for the better. Here are six ways to promote your own self-confidence.

1. ACT THE PART - Your body language can instantly demonstrate self-assuredness, or it can scream insecurity. Present yourself in a way that says you are ready to master or take command any situation. Hold your head high, sit straight up, gently bring our shoulders back to align your spine and look directly at the other person when interacting. Avoid a limp handshake and maintain good eye contact while someone is speaking to you.
2. DRESS THE PART - When you look better, you feel better. If you chose clothing and accessories that fit you well, suit

your industry and lifestyle, and make you feel good, this will automatically increase your self-esteem. Look like the part you want to play, or in other words, suit up for success. Don't be afraid to let your personality shine in your accessories. Bold jewelry can be a focal point and a good conversation starter.

3. SPEAK ASSERTIVELY - The next time you listen to your favorite speaker, be mindful of the way he or she delivers a speech. A great speaker speaks with confidently, in a steady rhythmic tone. Instead of the "ums" and 'ahs' that interrupt the flow, they use pauses to emphasize ideas.

4. THINK AND ACT POSITIVELY - Positive energy leads to positive outcomes, so set your mind to the can-do side of any situation, avoiding the negative self-talk that can make you feel less confident. Smile, laugh and surround yourself with happy positive people. You'll feel better and the people with whom you work will enjoy your company.

5. TAKE ACTION - There's more to being confident than just how you look. You must act the part. Walk up to a stranger at a networking event, or accept a project you'd normally reject. Practice being self-confident and soon it will become second nature. Jot down your strengths and weaknesses, but use what you've got and capitalize on your strengths instead. Once you put more energy into your positive traits, your confidence will start to shine through.

6. BE PREPARED - Remember the five P's: Prior planning prevents poor performance. The more prepared you are, the more confident you'll feel about your expertise and competency. Preparation will help you avoid getting tripped up by life's unexpected glitches. Learn everything you can about your industry, your subject matter, your goals, and what drives you towards success. Don't try to accomplish too much at once. Break complex tasks up into small, bite-size manageable pieces.

So when you walk in confidence, it will definitely show. It will also show the level of stature you are at as well. She will speak well; she will speak clearly and with assertiveness. Walk with your head held high, in that it will clearly say that you are looking above your potential. If you walk with your head held down, it may signal that you are looking beneath your potential.

KNOWING WHO YOU REALLY ARE

The Bible says in Psalm 139:14 NIV: "I praise you because I am fearfully and wonderfully made; your works are wonderful and I know that full well." According to your new character and consciousness, you must embrace yourself. Know thy worth, love thy self, and don't settle for less than you deserve. You must know there is a place called Promise. A woman who knows who she is in Christ, does not react but she respond.

That's why you have to watch who's leading you; allow your God-consciousness to kick in. Remember, your spirit is saved but your eyes, body, and mind isn't. I must respond to you by giving you a compliment. That's why I don't roll my eyes at you because God might bless me with a nicer outfit, you see? You uplift your counterpart, your sister. Encourage, Empower, Embrace, and Edify her and yourself to get yourself to the next level in Christ.

Also, keep in mind that God made no one like you; you are the only one with your finger prints. You're the one with the blueprint to your destiny. Of what you can become and make of yourself lies within you. You be the interior designer of your inner spirit and the architect of your outer exterior.

YOUR THOUGHT PATTERN

It's all in our thought pattern, because my thoughts become my actions and my actions become my destiny. Or, thoughts will become imaginations, then imaginations become strongholds. Thoughts are stored, then it becomes a mindset, then it becomes cement. You can't stop thoughts from coming but you can stop them from dominating. You also can't stop a bird from flying over your head but you can stop him from building a nest over your head. When you get filled with the Holy Spirit, you have to have enough ammunition inside of you to master your thoughts and mindset. Don't have a simple mindset. Because you have to learn how to plan and process. Do you have a small mindset, a selfish mindset? You need the right mindset – and that mindset is the mind of Christ. Amen.

SCRIPTURE'S TO OVERCOME

Overcome To Pray
Psalm: 86: 1-7
Matthew 6: 5-13
Romans 8:26
Hebrews 4:16
Jeremiah 33:3

Overcomer To What God Wants
Isaiah 42: 16
Psalm 32: 8
John 16: 13
James 1: 5
Proverbs 3: 5,6

Overcome To Forgive Others
Luke 6: 7
Matthew 6: 14,15
Mark 11: 25,26
Ephesians 4: 31,32
Colossians 3: 12,13

Overcome Depression
Revelation 2: 4
Isaiah 61: 1-3
Philippians 4: 8,9
Psalm 34: 6
Jeremiah 31: 25

Overcoming To Giving Into Temptation
John 16: 33
Romans 8: 37
James 1: 2,3

1 Corinthians 10: 3
Luke 22: 31,32

Overcoming Marital Problems
Genesis 2: 18
Proverbs 10: 12
1 Peter 1: 22
Proverbs 31: 10-31
Ephesians 5: 22-28

DEDICATION

I dedicate this book to the two women that are my heroes and my angels. My late mother and sister, Mrs. Mary Frances Wilson and Mrs. Belinda Jean Mikell. My mother birthed, guided, and nurtured me, but my sister taught me. You are part of the reason why I am the woman that I am today. I never knew or could have ever imagined that my life would have turned out the way it did after your passing and feeling alone once you two departed this earth. I think of you every day of my life. Momma, you left this earth when I needed you most and tears flow every time I think of you.

I would like to thank you, my mother and sister, for teaching me the essentials of life. How to cook, clean, dress like a woman, how to love the right way, be a mother, and pay my bills. You taught me the important roles in life such as how to be the best woman I possibly could be. But most of all how to exalt the Father, our Lord and Savior, Jesus Christ. Nothing will bring you back to this life but as I learn to live on without you. You will always be in my heart and hold a special place in my life. I want the world to know that you two special women have mapped out the road that I walk today. I still look to you as my role models because you've imparted so much in me and it is now that I pour out and am giving back to you with this autobiography of my life. I miss you both so very much. No one will ever understand the love I have for you. Thank you for all you have done for me, your grandsons, and nephews. God knew what was best when he put you two at rest. You will forever be in my heart and it has been a blessing experiencing life as your daughter and sister. I close this dedication but never my love.

Love,
Your Daughter and Sister,
Anjela D. Anderson

In Loving Memory

Mary Frances Wilson
July 24, 1939 - March 5, 2008

Belinda Jean Mikell
July 3, 1956 - July 2, 2009

Printed in the United States
By Bookmasters